PRAISE FOR *GREEN FOR LUCK*

"The effervescence and allure of Margaret Yapp's debut collection *Green for Luck* is her keen intuition to be both playfully sharp and delicately discerning. *Green for Luck* contains a beautiful balance of chorus and refrain from a poet whose confidence and ease propels the collection's neoteric coolness and observant nerve. What is to be said to a poet who writes of being shy, of being insecure, of being self-aware, of being loved, of seeking or finding god – in lovers or friends or her dog—Yapp's writing is not so mischievous as it is appreciative. Her ability to be her own lover is the collection's true centerfold. Since first reading Margaret Yapp's poetry several years ago, I find myself returning to lines that have surfaced and resurfaced as this collection has reached its final form: "as this body bloom / this body's knot". Whether from the reverbs of "DUMP TINKER" or "PUTTER PINE", or the playwrighting feature of "C", each piece in this collection has the power of pulse to both charm and strike, reminding the reader that Yapp is in control."

—m.s. REDCHERRIES
author, *Mother*

"Margaret Yapp is a poet who will not allow me to forget her. When she writes, "I get off on finding meaning," she means it. When she refers to her poems as "inside jokes with myself rotated by familiar angles," I believe her. And I laugh anyway. She's so funny and obsessive and aware. I have to imagine she encounters the world much as a raccoon does—curiously, hungrily, and with her hands, holding it close, turning it over in her weird little fingers until its bumps and peculiarities tell her the story she's feeling it for. Somehow, her poems manage to be both unbearably precise and unimaginably wild. Each time I read them, I find myself chasing a voice too slippery and alive to ever actually be caught, a voice given to playfulness and mischief, but also to tenderness, to examination, to deep attention and all the ways sound and light and feeling determine the shape of a life. In other words, *Green for Luck* is a good book. I think only Margaret could have written it."

—STEVEN DUONG
author, *At the End of the World There is a Pond*

PRAISE FOR *GREEN FOR LUCK*

"Margaret Yapp's *Green for Luck* is a precocious, bold first book. It is a fun, honest read that's not afraid to be, literally, "all over the place", all over the page. It encourages us to explore our dramatic, grounded, "messy" versions of home, steadfastness and curiosity. In these pages you will find inquiries into the self and what the self is made of, with unblinking truth and joy."

—TRACIE MORRIS
author, *human/nature poems*

"*Green for Luck* begins with a list of fields: "...the field familiar, the field by a lake, the field with no gate..." The open field, the unified field, the field of American poetry: in this warped and lucid debut, Margaret Yapp prances across all the fields, making her strange, shimmering music. These poems bend the page, break idioms, demand that you stop and study their erratic orbits. I kept asking myself: where my eyes should be, how do I read these poems? Delirious, the delight of being so disoriented: I emerged from *Green for Luck* with my sense of reading—of poetry itself—reseeded, remade, renewed."

—TOBY ALTMAN
author, *Discipline Park*

"Threaded across each deceptively playful litany in *Green for Luck* is a treatise about what it could mean to both be and feel good now: "The world's literally on fire & we were born into the middle. The middle of / the light. I'm distracted & busy waiting for a text back." We're falling asleep on the couch at the end of a party, the conversation slipping deliciously into the next room. A descendant of everything the sound poets meant by "field," *Green for Luck* reinvigorates the page as a limit through modes of witness that know the screen but turn towards the page. A simmering debut. A book equal parts landscape and singing bowl."

—SARAH MINOR
author, *Slim Confessions*

GREEN FOR LUCK

poems

Margaret Yapp

Green for Luck

Margaret Yapp

ISBN 978-1-958094-52-5

POETRY

COVER DESIGN   ALANA SOLIN

EastOver Press encourages the use of our publications
in educational settings. For questions about
educational discounts, contact us online:
www.EastOverPress.com or info@EastOverPress.com.

PUBLISHED IN THE UNITED STATES OF AMERICA BY

Rochester, Massachusetts
www.EastOverPress.com

GREEN FOR LUCK

THE LIST OF FIELDS THE LIST OF

fields goes like this : practice field, field with the hostas,
field by the lake, the familiar field, the field with no gate,
field with a thorough bottom, the field similar to familiar,
over there! The field of your own wrist.

The vegetation, though not thick, is beautiful—
the goodness supple as gloves, the vacant lot.

The face of each field is distinct & visible : a reflection
toward you, sound, striking

GOOD LIAR BAD LIAR

I believe in luck, only the good kind. I believe in ghosts, only
the good time in case you missed it. In case you missed it
magnolia can grow in Iowa too & plants can do something
close to what I might spell "talking" & I believe in talking
to oneself or myself. Ring the new bluebells none,
a pearl jest, leaky system, leaky gut, rot, drops,
my friend saying "so you were talking about your body?"
             Come over & repeat back to me everything I say

to you like a planet longing, like a planet yawning.

      I'm sick of this song, onto the next one. Carbon, water, signals, sugars move subterranean circuits. Garlic is soooo sticky sometimes! The great onion of consciousness is hard to kill & easy to scare. Over the last 200 years, in some places, the amount of time a drop of rain remains on the landscape has shortened from centuries to mere days. Brown sugar will harden when its natural moisture evaporates. To re-soften sugar, pour into microwave-safe bowl & cover with moist paper towel, set microwave to high, zap in 20 second increments til it smells like the mall.

      Obviously I wonder about you & the eggplant will need to be used by tomorrow & the greens. I'll go for ego murder unless nurture sounds better? Nature?

ALL ANGELS

balance small, across
from the toilet, living room,
bowing in her bedroom, many
above doorways ....

                        the word "angel" comes
                        from the word "messenger"
                        & I love her an abundance of messages!

& our laughter & how we go & go & go & go

I'm shorthand to indignant without her.

Our concordance echoes
good morning & good life
our working thread :
                        I adore her & she knows it.

                    There's an ending with nothing unsaid.

CONTENT

ROUND

so far
the light everything.
There are folds
　　　overlapping, adjusting to collect,
　　　　　capture the light.

　　　　　　I wish the center & I wish the list
　　　　　　I am the gravel & I am the fish.
Indices
　　　suggest
I'd like to redo everything ....
　　　　　does that check out?
Grab on
　　to
　　excuse or exercise.
Mushrooms may signal heart rot
　　　　(spores ingest heart wood)
hormone sentence for
　　　　over score
　　　　　or under story

　　　　　　till the swing up
　　　　　　super flower
　　　　　　super flower

THE GUT

insist the sky looks

       different here.

Pissed & eager, downstairs dreamer, body by chronic IBS.

    Pan, cast iron.
    Ferritin, deficient

rage cleaning, earnest. Heard us, to a high

       appoint a finger away from
       myself toward not myself.

    In the shower this morning
    I found two quinoa in my buttcrack hair

       (overcooked for sure
        & I'm okay with that)

       the stimulus of thought & motion

          root suckers grow with & sideways
        particular presence of rays & crystals.

The light, heat held in hand, I'm hungry
                      hungry hungry hungry.

I have opinions,
I'm making choices : grab a wad of napkins
    big enough to fill the glove compartment.

      History of courtroom illustrators, mudrooms.

Thoughtful throttle, bucket lifestyle, the light everything.

     It feels good to walk
     with my righteous catalog of grievances
         right here in my pocket.

        One use of eyeliner is to repel the sun

STONE SKIPPING

histories of lie detection :
boiling water
hot piece of metal
dry bread & hard cheese
magic & divine forces
cold water
rice in mouth
consecrated meal
handwriting peculiarities

The galvanometer, an important part
of the polygraph lie detector
was invented in the late 1700's by an astronomer-priest.

Seriously, let go & let god ....

when attached by wires
through which electricity runs
the galvanometer will cause a needle to move
& a pen to trace paper

blood pressure change
breathing change
bioelectric skin reactivity
& other

                                    haughty go lucky
                                   mites in eyelashes
                         plot points in the lifeline of a hair.
                                            The light

              line splits the lawn
              reveals different habits.

Help I'm stuck in the drama triangle & I can't get out!

A room with carpet
                              a milky drink
                              a suggestion
                         in a hot month, tease, stub.

Watch how I lick
my sounds
                         & follow suit

(bleeding hearts, peonies, flock of shasta daisies)

I'm like

I'm like

I'm like

I'm like taking out my anger on anyone older than me.

       Yearn into
           signature font & baby
                  names.

          Stick the electrodes to the lilac sippy cups
                to see what's up
        are these blooms telling the truth or what?

       Moving a set of loops from one stick to another

          out strong, effort

                arrow, flank, butterfly.

DUMP

I can't believe I slept so little so often .... Sometimes my tampons go under .... which makes sense carrots? Swallow hard. Actually

DUMP   TINKER

seven planets to the light. My eyes hunker : glowing heart with half arrow on left side changes into an arrow pointing up right, back to half arrow heart, repeats. I notice some wallpapers eight eight eight .... quick trip stops. Right wind barrier left more lanes. I cross another violent invisible line into the field of opportunity going a little over. A window & a ladder stitched in front

TINKER

many days. I don't miss swimming or think about swimming
smell like a full Easter supper .... when I do, it's like memories
& very underslept. So, is this romantic? Let me guess baby
I'm nowhere in this dump & of course I do. Wheels stuck

PUTTER

I won't take for granted the small square window in our front
from. Making piece (fake piece) or faking piece, winning
closing up shop, they gossip, unionize. An empty rectangular
missing to crawl inside or thrust through. Or five blankets

door, where competition comes
action .... my pinky toes consider
parallel pipe, just enough sides
in a room. Here I am, I bow out

PUTTER

PINE

lantern bug, peanut bug, alligator bug. His mirror face. Cause to starve, away. I colander greens in the sink, wet my shirt, break the cup, spill a liquid, vibration through cord. Sharp quick ring of a vessel maker. Fluid, juice of animal, plant. Laughter, by definition, requires moisture remember? We spoke about this. To indulge a whim, an organized theory, universally recognized

PUSH PIN

metaphor comes from to carry over & ink from to burn in. Look back for what my friend says. Easy. Each motion is a field. Water becomes weight, soaks the skin to which she sticks a strip. A candle on top of a green house. Evidence succumbs interrupting notion, loves each field to echo.

A clinging voice can be dense or not. Dense as in stupid & tough to scrub away. Foot hold burns. Hold means & gravity, or money .... the rectangle is the fastest shape a human brain can process. Observation, sure to mind which room, which rearing .... a seed goes traveling & my guests leave

mud on my clog heel, mowing down creeping charlie. Well, that's not my house & not my grass!
I mean, I must. Dyed with lac, leave it there. Clogged pores, minor betrayals, holding what I hold.
Here, I'm talking windows, a green chair & a vase balanced on a detail. My bad toe as a weapon.

I'm here pooling armor & identity claims, clams, crabs walking in hot water. Attune, counter.
Hum out of order. The house I first had sex in has been for sale for like four years! Market Street.
The notion of capability goes "woo   woo   woo   woo"

THE LIGHT THE LIGHT THE LIGHT THE LIGHT

I'm trying to pray to god so I can stop thinking
about god & about the first uncut dick

I ever saw & tenderness. How tenderness
matters today & matters tomorrow.

I got a nosebleed during sex with a new lover.
I have an iPhone 6S & I'm covered in bruises.

I want to say I'm kinky but I'm just anemic.
The world's literally on fire & we were born

into the middle. The middle of the light.
I'm distracted & busy waiting for a text back.

What does "abject" mean?
I'm an animal in my middle.

Tenderness doesn't matter, only coincidence

MY LOVE LANGUAGE IS MID

weed yarrow redbud & browngrass prairie
snow snow snow snow & infinite crocus
all the way back to redbud & milkweed.
There are more : honeysuckle shrub & shrug,
the bloom we called honeysuckle for years
before we discovered better, prairie.
I want you to know how warm rain can come
& down petals during July's big storm.
Isn't this beautiful? Infinity—
redbud browngrass prairiefire : I want you
to know how it's nice to feel warm, crocus.
I want you to know I'm waiting for you
to come back to this place with seasons

INDECENT SONNET

seven words in we stop playing scrabble
to fuck on my living room floor : you turn
your pieces over : I leave mine alone
letters-up : E I I A O A O
only vowels : I have lost already.
I want you to turn me over too, please
please would you turn me over entirely?
Look! Look at my blood all over the quilt!
Luckily blood looks a lot like quilted
roses & to be beneath you is to
be beneath an idea of something
found. L U C K I L Y is a seven letter word
& F O R E V E R & Q U I L T E D & B E N E A T H!
Beneath you forever : I have only vowels

THE LIGHT THE LIGHT THE LIGHT THE LIGHT

I don't have time to pray. I'm busy
sending nudes to my contact list.

I don't know how to start a fire, only know why one
might end. Sex is only a small death if we actually come.

I'm addicted to wondering about my unconscious
& I continue & continue to try to find the light.

I pray to god for the light.
There's no reliable names. No matter how fast we burn

I wouldn't want to be caught in the middle
alone like this. From here on out I promise

I'm only going to let people hurt my feelings.
I'm an animal digging against my middle

& we can only witness from far away : the light

PANDER

findable, doesn't have location. Still I balk to ridge to bridges
run at best slightly sweet. Worst, tasteless. Glom onto steal
to pitch this ball without completion. Clam & trace lines
that someone else drew already, around them, between

PANDER

ding, dong, ditch, deckle. Pile where I've repeatedly kicked my boots then gone inside.

I'm certain about direction like a print stuck in brick. String & lines smaller than rope.

Dreams with great weight inside my arms, I fly sometimes. Tag, seven up, locks of hair.

I don't regret giving away my childhood rock collection. Tucker in reference to cloth or dogs

RIDDANCE

some information exists that isn't
& butterfly to bunny .... the nobs
an unplowed strip. A motion made
to great squeeze the pudding out

C (A PLAY IN THE MIDDLE)

CAST :

SHOULD SEE SIDEWAYS

SHOULD TWO PEOPLE, IF POSSIBLE

CHARACTERS :

SHOULD GIVE SUBTLE YET DISTINCT
EXPRESSION TOWARD MY OLD FRIEND,
A LOOK SHE'LL RECOGNIZE

CUE :

SHOULD SIGNIFY, NOD TO SUGGEST,
BUT NOT NECESSITATE AN AUDIENCE.
SHOULD POINT INTO, PRESUMING AN AUDIENCE.
IN CASE OF NO AUDIENCE,
SHOULD LOOK, SEE, WITH AN EXPRESSION
THAT BRINGS CLOSE TO LITERAL WARMTH
& A FEELING OF QUITE EARNEST BELONGING
TO THE AUDIENCE,
IF THERE IS AN AUDIENCE

C (A PLAY IN THE MIDDLE)

CAST :

"should listen & do"

"1. they have a moment, 2. in the backyard"

CHARACTERS :

"once, I asked this woman I had just met
what mascara she was wearing
because her lashes looked amazing
& she said 'I don't remember'...."

CUE :

ACT 1 : COY

DELIVER THE FIRST LINE, LOOK UP

TWIRL

LOOK TOWARD

"I'm shy I'm shy I'm shy I'm shy I'm shy"

A GESTURE SHOULD SIGNIFY

MUSTER FORWARD

ACT 1 : COY

"I'm at the dog park with three dogs, my job."

"Two geese circle the park above us .... twice
counter clockwise then twice clockwise. I watch
with one of the dogs. The other two dogs don't give a shit.
The other day I met my future self. She looks really good,
she looks like my mom, I love her."

"In a movie, I like unexplained synchronized dancing.
In a music video, I like over-acted facial expressions.
Scene idea for us to try : two women
saying 'I'm shy' in unison for eternity.

I'm shy I'm shy I'm shy I'm shy I'm shy
I like it when everything turns green, for luck."

"Bow, bowl, scowl, sorry, good point & well put.
Meaning unwilling to commit to the bit, rest, quiet.
Simper to affected, nibble, nibs, attending.
Tailor to cutting, twig."

"Select signage unlimited.
The shows I watch alone. Of course I look at those."

ACT 2 : CUD

KNIFE TUG BEYOND A STEM INTO THE YELLOW

OFFER TO SPLIT ONE

LAUGH TRACK

SLAP STICK

"knife tug beyond the center into another"

ACT 2 : CUD

"The geese are long gone by now, if it wasn't obvious.
I'm back home too, home from the dog park, back
with my own dog now. I drove while I was talking
about shyness & green. I drove on familiar streets
& a lucky color, hit it off, block rock weekend.
A specific eyes unfocus, a certain fuck it, growl, playlist."

"When it rains it pours, when it rains I'm wistful.
The winch related to wheel, pulley, wink. Yearn
seems more accurate than long."

"My old friend is out there somewhere & doing okay,
presumably, though I wouldn't know directly."

"No, no, I meant that in a chummy way!"

"Would I like to split one?
I consciously give my hands their rest."

"Thank god for glue sticks, nic sick. I like the obvious
joke someone has to say but it sucks & is brave
to be the one to actually say it. The wrong pipe
to hiss the pan I don't clean well."

ACT 3 : CRUX

"a noble pursuit"
EVAPORATE WITH REGULAR USE

SHRUG

DIALOGUE TO PROVE IT ALONG

VIM

BLESS, NEXT, ACT UP ON IT, INTO IT

ACT 3 : CRUX

"Literally any time, I like a montage. They work!"

"Yeah, I'm friendly & thoughtful .... so what?"

"An affair. The definition slipped somewhere else.
Heard of it? Take a sample, this bullshit
changed my life! But then there's what one has to do.
Ordinary business.
To do, make. To set, put.
To barefoot, rue."

"I've said it before, I'll certainly say it again : I like it
when everything turns green."

"I'm so into this.
A line about a line of blue light.
Fresh-mowed grass does smell really good
but there's nothing like driving
when the heat in my car starts working again.
Do I want a better story?
I'm just a few blocks away
from there, where, chokehold, my friend."

ACT 4 : COAX

"handkerchief, hankerchief"
HANKER, HANKER, HUNKER

SCOLD TO FAMOUSLY FEARED, CLAMOROUS

SHOOT SHOT, STAMMER, IT'S OKAY
TO REPRIMAND, RUBBERMAID, ROMPER,
TO SCOLD, STAGGER

SCOFF OUT BUT THE SCOFF
PUFFS THE CHEST

HEDGE BETS

ACT 4 : COAX

"Some days, touchpads don't notice my fingers."

"I know bettter."

"In a bad mood, invite my sense of scarcity, regret
a direction. Many hours, the same window."

"On edge, I would love to make a point.
I'm not competitive, I'm realistic.
I say to my dog on a just-us walk: 'you're so lucky
to have me, your dad would never let you act like this.'
There are many uses for the sound trunk. If I trace
long enough, every sound moves back toward wood
or similar. An intimate story at a quick pace in terms
of length of conversation or knowing one another.
Where do you tend to get off?"

"I got attacked by a dog & it became my whole personality
but just for a little while."

ACT 5 : CLAM

PERT

POACH MERINGUE

CURTSY TO DO OR MAKE A PLAYFUL LEAP OR
JUMP, A SKIP OR SPRING. PRANKS COME LATER
TO SPORTIVE ACTION, PETTY CRIME
"no worries"

SLINK, GRIEF, LOOK TO SEA

CRUISE CONTROL TO COUNTER, CONSIDERABLE

ACT 5 : CLAM

"Rectangles with space for echo .... I'm like a raw bone
some days & others? An early type of bicycle. Substance
to pick, as happy as fetter to string, drips, objects
& events. The dust that clings to ceiling fan blades.
Popularity contest, unfulfilling dinner party.
To sprinkle elementary substance, kick, detachable."

"When was competition invented?
Well .... the concept of confidence was invented
over 200 years ago. The concept of loneliness?
200 years before that! So I do the math!
History is so interesting!"

"I told flax, forge, scum, scut, goad to stick.
One of the many things one can fix with a fingernail!"

"May be the cause, at any event, a sense
of vague proceedings. Dump, still, to dough
& here, a misunderstanding between dawn,
that's fine, direct copy, whatever."

ACT 6 : CAPER

LATCH LIKE INTO GEAR
LIKE ON A BIKE, LIKE THE LATCH OF ASLEEP

"pleasure & a little extra"

ALWAYS IMPRESSIVE,
TINY, PRECISE, REPETITIVE
MOVEMENTS, GET ALONG

CRAMP, FETTER

ACT 6 : CAPER

"In a plot, I don't mind a hinged box
as some sort of metaphor or constriction,
or just a prop, even. I like boxes. They're useful
for holding things, storage."

"What happens at the end
of forget me not? My own medicines.
I know they're mine
because of the certain stains.
Where we eat
& take in through senses."

"How old is this back? Connected to wheel, ruche
to beehive, bark, straw. Frozen whipped cream.
I'm on the pot. I like 'been too long' shortened
to 'too long' & 'close to the chest' or better yet, 'vest'."

"When a character is watching another sleeping character
& the first character finally walks away
& then the second character opens their eyes, revealing
they were, in fact, awake the entire time ....
I'm into that."

CUT

GENUINE SCENE, TWO SIDES,
STRATEGIC CUT.
THE TWO PEOPLE, IF POSSIBLE
SHOULD MOVE IN CONCENTRIC
CIRCLES FOR A LITTLE WHILE
DIFFRACTING IN ACCORDANCE
WITH TAPED INSTRUCTIONS

SHOULD LOOK IN FRIEND'S
GENERAL DIRECTION
OR WHEREVER
FRIEND IS, LOOKING

"are there two people?"

GO ON

CUT

"I believe in God because soooo many times I'll think
about someone & two hours later they'll text me."

"Anyway, if it was in fact true ....
that this woman applied mascara that very morning ....
because it was early in the day when we met ....
through my friend & she couldn't remember the brand ....
well then I simply can't relate."

"I'm at an exhibition at the costume council.
I know why I'm here & where I am
which is nice & a relief.
The clarity. The relief
of leaving a place to be elsewhere.
Even when the reason is inability.
I feel good getting older, I feel familiar."

ACT 7 : COIL

CHECK THE CARPET,
STAY HOME & CHECK THE CARPET

"foundational NPR memory"

BREAK, PEEL, SPECK, SPOT, COME OFF

ACT 7 : COIL

"Where's my needle & my other needle?"

"I ponder feeling my alone time. My alone time
in the mornings. My alone time walking. My alone time
walking in a list of every other place I've lived.
My alone time on my way to meet someone."

"There are things I have forgiven because of beauty.
I'm picking up my dog's poop, neighbor dog is freaking out,
I say to neighbor dog: 'it's okay, you're okay'
I don't mind a mid performance, it's fun!"

"Dead horses are really sad & also movies
about missed connections specifically because of logistics.
Detour due to construction pushes me past the street
I grew up on. Thought .... feeling .... behavior ....
did you get that? This song is misplaced. Karaoke
to get bigger, emptied pit, I prefer a private room.
Which weight will be enough? I'm talking blankets.
Thumb nail through the strawberry greens.
Paints, oils, glass, pallets. A blade or a bed, both tools
with maximum width. Measure my carry on by eye,
then ruler, then scale. The act of watching, to gather
into rings, one above the other."

ACT 8 : CRUDE

FAKE IT, FADED

INCLUDE A VAGUELY-MISPLACED,
COMMONLY-ENOUGH-USED
PHRASE SO THE PHRASE FEELS VAGUELY OFF
BUT IT'S IMPOSSIBLE TO SAY WHY

INTO IT

CLAMBER

"off track"

ACT 8 : CRUDE

"Crushed like a hit weight, hard, wreck, reck & righteous."

"Here I'm wondering if I'm in on it.
Indignant & in on it. Resentment
is a back pocket solution but I love to be right.

"I'm so good at texting. It's not my fault ....
we had fantastic typing education in middle school.
I have skills! I've worked out before!
Walking away with my hands full.
Are we all wearing clogs this weekend?"

"Most of this is just us not being able
to hear each other on the phone."

"It's too bad about asthma ....
shortness of toes, tuft, thatch, inherited.
I'm in my hometown hoping to run into someone
specific & I like my alone time
only when there's lust outside."

ACT 9 : CRAB

HARD HAT

PUT THE HAT ON, AT LEAST FOR A WHILE,
OR FINALLY EXPERIMENT WITH GLOVES

LEGGED & PRESSED INTO A STICK & MISTAKE

STUBBORN, SHOULD STUBBORN
GET INTO TROUBLE

CHUMP TO BLOCK OF WOOD, BLOCK-HEADED

"a gesture"
AT THE AUDIENCE
IF THERE IS AN AUDIENCE)

ACT 9 : CRAB

"I'm into physical comedy & I said I'm shy, not timid."

"That's the girl that threw a hammer at her sister!"

"I'm obsessed with thoughts
that another has obviously had before.
I'm down with presumptions
& I love a cartoon cutaway gag!"

"Fog I feel physically, I'm talking actions. I'll wipe my
hands on whatever. All animals are stubborn."

"I like it when a character says the name of the show
within dialogue & everyone in the audience cheers.
It's so sad when a genuinely funny person makes a joke
that they *didn't* have to say. I got my eyes checked today
& they're just vaguely fucked, see?"

ACT 10 : COWLICK

HYPBERBOLE PAST

"deck change"

COVER, STENOGRAPHER,
PIGEON HOLE, FURTHER FOR ITS OWN SAKE

STRAFE, PUT ON

SHARP, HORIZONTAL BACK & FORTH
OF THE HEAD, AGAIN. PRICE MATCH
ON TOYS, BOOGERS, PIMPLE PATCHES,
SEBACEOUS FILAMENTS, BIRTHDAY CAKE
"a painting qualifies when detail dictates time"

ACT 10 : COWLICK

"A group of people engaging in a discussion
about television & which pastries look good.
In just about anything, I want
a will-they-won't-they .... they-will."

"Effort that's mine to spend, float in between
attending toward various materials."

"'I remember' is always redundant."

"When we walk down my childhood block,
I sense my dog can talk to my dead childhood dog.
They don't talk about me."

"I barely remember the flood from my teenage years.
Like it's erased from my memory. I once asked
my old friend if she remembered the flood
& she said of course, she sandbagged for weeks."

ACT 11 : COUCH

"or couch, I wonder?"

SEE, AT THE TOP OF THE TOWER,
GREEN IN THE MIDDLE

WAVE GREEN FLAG
DESPITE THIS FENCE, FIGURES, FINGERS

MOUTH, FINGERS UN-CROSSED
"Two living things connected by a length of fabric"

BOW TO FORWARD PART OF THE SHIP

"open eyes under"

ACT 11 : COUCH

"Fruit of a wild apple tree, scratch, carve, not
just sound, space or distance. An unexpected
yet understandable & pleasurable pitch change.
Nothing beats good timing."

"Here's your hat what's your hurry?"

"I beg my dog to never die."

"Two living things connected by a length of fabric."

"This is not absence since one at a time I meet
circumference."

"A soft close versus hard close, I'm talking doors.
How often has a lover formed this light?
Yes, quietly, a distinct line, a great rectangle.
Our front window tells me important things.
Same difference, open to somewhere else.
Sour, reflected. I mean color, effected."

ACT 12 : CRUSH

GO DOUBLE SLOW, OPEN EYES UNDER

"open eyes under water"

"open eyes under two short doors"

"or two bodies tangled with a bench"

ACT 12 : CRUSH

"I ran into my old friend's parents at the grocery store.
I had dreamt about this moment a few times
so I told them so, though the dreams
took place at a different grocery chain.
I told them this too.
I hugged them each once.
I asked them to tell my old friend 'hi'
& I resited the urge to pass on other information."

"I'll take a bite-sized piece, suitable to be held
in a cheek. To put in possession, not in a stage
of contingency, a thing that signifies impending
positive effort, complicated effort,
last-minute cancellation & no regret.
A thimble of any, a thimble of up, over, toward
dogwood tree & shrub, street or cul-de-sac.
A re-named street, anonymous in the old sense."

"I love my mornings. I'm thinking, I'm talking....
this specific exchange for example: two bells held
up with green, dripping water,
or two bodies tangled with a bench."

(CURTAIN)

"the light the light

should let the light

a renamed object

should look to the audience

the light the light

bow again, wipe
an eye, then the other,
nose, for good measure,
to signify that feeling
of earnest belonging"

(CURTAIN)

"fly, net

the light on a wall

bow out

in the middle

call

if there is an audience

to out, strong, effort"

tickle of sugar shell. Loud, clear, ringing sound. This is the last time I'll mention them .... birds who live in malls. Actually don't trust me. A satellite object tins. Root is usually sex & I'm okay with that .... excited about that, even. A wall hides a beam, a ceiling hides a beam. Imagine exposing all that. Hope has a mass, it's over there! A place beyond covers hope's whole surface

SYNC

away. Taste is about alternation who caters lusts off other, under deep fall, gut, lot, a regular old can be made with the materials

SWALLOW

there's wax in here! Milk from a countable number of miles
(my humble theory) . I lament, awl, influenced by an agent
panders a base passion oily & the greens. Mum's ability into
part of a curved line bows birdlime & a sticky time bomb

HERE ARE ANIMALS

not so long ago everything was gigantic,

opposite of a map,

some say miraculous.

We hadn't yet committed to round or flat.

There were animals in the oceans, animals in the trees,

animals just beginning.

It's not easy to love what doesn't want to be found.

Animals eat only at night.

Animals hunt in shadows forever

for at least one answer.

We demand bones and video evidence.

Instead we find shit stuck to the bottoms of our shoes.

We wonder about plausibility.

It becomes clear animals are very good at hiding,

life is not romantic & animals don't need us

to stretch far as stars

NAB

as this seed body
bloom sulfur & carbon
& calcium for breakfast
& this light body
bloom grape & vine
around for sulfur lunch

& this water body
bloom wheat for dinner

I'm searching
exact measurements for time

as this body bloom
this body's knot

LAUNDROMAT SEXTING

so hot you believe in god
belief shows you're capable of worship.

                Hot machines simultaneously cleaning
                  beliefs we have in every stubborn god.
                    Belief's capability in stubbornness.

My iPhone 6S autocorrects "dildo" to "fulfill"
it's so romantic here on earth.
We can spread our butter
on our bread, we can eat.

                    I want to know what kind of worship
                          tick worship
                        lick each branch
                every leaf all leaves worship?

I'm out of soap
wondering if you're anyone
with capability.

                    Legs clinging each branch worship.
I heard a rumor there's a lot of water on the moon ....
                        can I do laundry at your place?

CASINO

can you bring me to a casino in the middle of nowhere
& let's see what happens in a place where nothing is
embarrassing anymore? My backup

horoscope app calls this life "the loner's path."
I'm seeking any working hot tub.
An eagle flies outside my window nowhere close to a river
so I ask my phone "does that mean anything?"

Horoscope app answers "shut the fuck up about birds"
but I get off on finding meaning
like sudden death soybeans
next to the casino parking lot.

Like how flood water busts empty space & emptiness
inevitably return : return : return : returns

WATER NOT WEATHER

singing across river
I can hear   see body
hair that keeps turning over
          the shoulder.
      I cannot see face.
Sometimes calls.
           Liver leaf.
Wine color.
    Lobed in odd number.
A face
         a gesture
expanding & contracting
       like a balloon

or a bone
      in boiling water

boiling   water

reeking

        of booze

OVER CORRECT

attent

delight the light. Catch
& go away with chest. Back

to squash
a bug
don't tell!

Requesting promises double
my very understandable
loss of memory & emphasis.

I sent magnolia petals in an envelope
to you across state lines

able, that

by the time the message reached you, the flower
had crisped the envelope brown, crusting

that that strike familiar

GUST

many quick consecutive exhales
accordion. Nipples the color of
a shrewd & open village like we
balance .... like crab to crabbed

GUST

POSIT

where sanctity comes from. An image sorted into five frames. Core that heart the innermost heart wrecked of uncertain origin. From tree or soil, a central portion cut, removed. Internal mold casting space intended. Quoted name : "hollow voice" which echos & that look between roommates. I saw someone on the street that was like a younger version of someone else I know sticking to the back back back back of throat. Sound through frozen strawberry. Clever. From out of a hinge, two horses joked, settled, rested inside. Jar on a pane, weight on a jar like dog from dogged, calf from calved. Pare split off, splinter

HUNKER

clocks protect cells from heat, from sun, posture, & position
my pinched nerve is a design flaw. Recognize click, recognize
jokes on hat, t-shirt, cup, or wing. The only human cell visible
a radius the tip of a pencil. Here I attempt to tell a story

GLOM

easy mistake .... metal for meat
click, recognize click. Timeless
with the naked eye is this, an egg
& the meaning hits you harder

HUNKER

I wonder how "thrust" & "push" have come to signify wasted time even around one's own home. My putter, for example, is amazing. We're both impressed by my miles in circle. That circle hitched to the top of our spines. A chiropractic up, out, & together. Electrical stimulation patches surround the bones in approximate measurement. I'm looking to flirt & see cool outfits

MAKE ME WAIT

act, snatch, regret, float, middle

from multiple sources
slurring at bottom

or so I thought

of course, I still
wonder about you & the greens
off their feet (chives)
chide, choke up on it

actually, good
regret
float
middle

at pretend,
I snatch
a print
from pressure

hard won, sexy, not impressed
(kissed)

FRET

curse, coaster, coozie
(the direction changes, not the current)

ultimately for & eat
(correct & heat)

trellis
to three threads, as if

god thought up a gesture just for me.
It's very possible I've seen this movie before ....
no need to cut til need to cut.

Everyone's giving me a little too much space ....
Oh! I made it myself!

Turd to split, to skit off, scoot over!
Can't shake, crisp, cluck

related to flight, of the earth in earthquakes.
Underneath transitioned to the whole of it.
Country, district to sphere,

use in old chemistry

MY CHIPPED TOOTH FEELS GOOD
LIKE A SECRET

scour the cloth, clog to lump of wood to large jewelry, knotty
log. Anything impeding action is the enemy or constitutes
dear encumbrance. The first example, a large animal, pick
one. Soot to perspective to drawing objects or appropriate
relation to optics. Copper, hinder, fasten, lie prostrate. Prone.
Of course I wanted a surprise & didn't get one. Choke up
with extra matter. I'm talking gutter, leaves, classic. Spout,
furrow, born from the shell of a goose. I didn't mean to
mention them again but I said don't trust me, oysters,

great rafts, consequently. Parallel
lines, loop holes spread into mud.

> Readily as glaciers, tiny blocks, acres & yet I don't go
> lineated, forms, a great light. Soundless green line,

velocity, duration, extent

WORLD ANGEL LOGISTICS

Mouths come ponderous, refracted
classified according to sub & emerge.
Drowned topography, wax, wave, part
of the weed. Corners are so exciting.
I'm talking seaweed, force, direction.
Missives formed in a sort of old way.
Systematically. I love a high budget
drama, a full up parking lot, a glass
of water, a pile of leftover dead leaves

        & I'll miss my chipped tooth
        like a secret, like a time of day,
        civilized. Or amount of time passing

knee deep! Needles fold & the records remain lifted,
little upon it, an unsure measurement toward intent

              to shun the name of a road,
       previous notion, previous conception,
              yearn to pretend the map.
              I considered the main forces
                that produce tides
      & I wonder if you know your effect

big bad bangs, phenomenon of the material world. Warm funnel cake & many dozen eggshells. What are the flowers like waxy doorknobs that won't open until ants chew through the sugar? Eggshells on the ceiling, I'm looking up there. Eggshells on the ground, I'm walking around them.

The courage to know splits in half, the difference cold & crusting. A train through several hoops. My friend told me the ant thing is a myth, peonies just want attention. A cube melts into roots. Gluestick the doorbell underneath it's house & a jar on it's comfortable side for sleeping, exactly

WELL DONE

I spend my forgetfulness on this condition of altitude .... I can't be sure of my memory's quality.
Noon's vast & my twin furrows steady, sheep. A wide awareness of periphery depends on memory.
Accused in fashion, what makes creaky flight. NEEDED : small familiar object just out of reach.

Well-adjusted like a weapon & well-adjusted as a weapon .... my good behavior as a weapon.
Forgiveness & my bulged disc as weapons. I'll describe to anyone where rolling eyes come from.
This is the back of my head, scuttle   scuttle   scuttle   scuttle

LATCH

DARN

Capability that feels good with crop corn rooming, where else to go. Ribbed text. Pants.

Mouth held specific to snug, fathom to full, a message mirror, ring, grin. Lined from one.

One night into doubles. Bottom third unscaled, so far unfilled, outline of a curved weight.

I'm fond to foolish of thick ground cover, affect until movement, ton, hills rough & rolling

LATCH

Riven or riddanced lengthwise.
Peat fuels in the earliest sense.
Make wet & quick work of that.
I am sure like a planet gnawing.

DARN

A finished shape. When riding, we need more length, breath.
Squishy considered a piece cut off. Various states of undress.
Unfortunately, I further a rip in our nice sheets with my heel.
A planet, dawning. Back wash, music, blow drying clingwrap.

SPOKE

There's skin cells in here! A heap & a hill, summit, backbone.
Origin appoints when a thing becomes impossible to interpret.
Crabapples .... they're bitter, there are lots of them, nice jam.
I'm on my couch where our dog is. She's running in her sleep.

DIRECT   SPOKE

rock deposits through some ice. Glacial erratics become sum, none, the fields & singular.

Here I am & I'm justifying through erratics. Inside jokes with myself rotated by familiar angles.

I like to listen to you explain what it was like to leave a certain location at a certain time of day.

I want you to meet me at any corner, center, store or fish hook. Like a cherry to pulpy drupe

DIRECT

I famously love this location ....

Crabgrass refers its very own self.

Its very small & crooked form.

I know when I know, a gesture.

HOT GOSSIP

suet

> perhaps
> perhaps perhaps
> I can do something similar
> enough with peanut butter.
> Making mud houses.
> Glossy, thistle, finally
> my favorite jelly beans.

Pity is delicious but what about a little risk for once?

Oh my pride .... my vanity .... I love those guys ....

commute flavor, commit favors,
easy on the teeth

fire resistant does not mean it will not burn

> bristle, want
> an expensive coat & applause
> carrying
> the past & ability
> Who woulda thunk?

There it is in the wash, indignant.
Liquid science of resent, reck, righteous

> less, trip, wash

one drop of acetone to re-thin nail polish turned

                              thick & goopy, shake well
the light everything

            file room & nail away
            let's stay inside for MODERN RESEARCH

                                          onto
            glacial erratics

                        many many many many folds.

                                    Quick Q actually!

                        Great onion ....

                              right on time to hide
                                    my water,
                              a real piece of work

            nip, wedge, remote, pine.

Four out of five animals on earth
are tiny soil worms turning waste into nutrients

soil, skin of living world
soil takes thousands of years to form

worms & string cut
sap seeps from cut
trying to remove the glass
from the table without spilling
every drop
on the side
of the room
with most of the light.

Salt fixation
salt fertility
salt reaction

gathering, dragging, the only rock I eat

I need a foot rub hard hard hard hard

humming humming still the string

cornflower bugs, fairy bugs, giant strawberry
& physical flavor

sister houses

wedge cuts

ants hilling on cement ....

how deep do you guys go anyway?

Bare naked lilies in our yard

& the wisdom to know the difference.

Manipulation of the light   good grievance

good riddance

good luck

bad day

(it's weird my mom & my dog don't really hang out.

I hope my dog knows how much I love her)

carbon sink

earth hook

sleep hook

sleep drip

sleep drop

sleep pop

sleep drop

elastic matters for elastic matters

life experiencing itself

I hope hope is reasonable

(twice removed hope)

a hat yet to be invented

an herby soup I've yet to try

relationship between the light

no belt, a waist, no belt, a waist

(ultimately I would do anything)

saying "we are now where we will always be"

delight the light
                    the light the light the light

alive

                  intention to be measured in spaces
        attention & direction   in & of

        along   expand

                     keeping in mind

                      circular time
             & every shape my brain
                  cannot imagine
my ultimate concern :

               surprise irises in my yard

                as good a word as any

geologic memory, long memory, long light, deep heat

OPEN WIDE

pin in it, water pick
me. In the plot I'm picking
nibbled cabbages

                                                        I ptui ptui

                                                        I can tell

from deer? Bunny? Despite
this fence, fights
from spit, hassle

                            wrestle   tension

                                spree   hard

I can hear one
above through

                          I can smell a home
                          haircut by the ears

by the skylight,
but I didn't say anything

                          from a mile away!
                    Where that shirt comes from

my tummy audible,
that unnecessary zipper

                          approximated lisp
                           a trace line

           of light through sky then glass then cloth.

ACKNOWLEDGMENTS

I don't know how to list all of the people who have helped me make this book. Friends, teachers, editors, collaborators, classmates, etc. There are many people to thank and as I've tried to write this list, this list has kept growing. Here's my attempt:

Some of these poems were lucky enough to be published previously, in their earlier forms, in: *TILT, Tupelo Quarterly, Second Factory, Asphalte, Driftwood, Brink, Annotations, Afternoon Visitor, Biscuit Hill, the lickety~split, New Delta Review, Post Road Magazine, Cutleaf Journal, mojo magazine, Peach Mag, mercury firs, Tyger Quarterly, Annulet,* and *the minnesota review*. Thank you to those editors and readers for their support.

My forever gratitude to everyone at EastOver for believing in this book and bringing it here.

Special thanks to Keith Pilapil Lesmeister. You have been my teacher, mentor, and friend for a decade and I wouldn't be where I am today without that.

Thank you, thank you, thank you Sarah Minor for the edits, guidance, and inspiration.

Thank you to my teachers Tracie Morris, Elizabeth Willis, Karen Carcia, Sara Langworthy, Amy Weldon, Athena Kildegaard, Diane Scholl, and Beth Fettweis.

I'm so lucky to have friends to send screenshots of google documents back and forth with. Thank you to my poet friends, my writer friends, to anyone who has ever offered notes on a poem, who has ever collaborated on a project, who has ever shared your work with me. Thank you especially: Sarah Adler, Adedayo Agarau, Amy Benfer, Madison Bennett, Emily Chan, Moriana Delgado, Dana King, and Jessie Kraemer for your friendship and your influence on my work. Thank you Ian Carstens, Henry Goldkamp, Serena Solin, and Tramaine Suubi for writing early reviews. Thank you Toby Altman, Steven Duong, and m.s. RedCherries for taking the time to read early on and for writing blurbs.

Thank you Alana Solin, my dear friend, for reading everything one million times. You are my partner in poetry and I'm beyond grateful. And of course, thank you for this amazing cover.

Thank you to John Downer for creating this beautiful Iowan Old Style typeface.

ACKNOWLEDGMENTS

Thank you to all of my friends, forever.

Thank you to my family. I'm nothing without you, apart from you. My moms Bridget and Kathleen, my dad John, my siblings James, Jack, and Grace, my aunt Kristi and uncle Milan, my cousins Steven, Elijah, Mikey, and Marco. My grandparents Jo, Jim, Joan, and Bill. My great grandma Jane who wrote poems. Breanne and Jess. My extended family. Thank you.

Thank you to my dog.

Thank you Trevor - half of this book is stuff you've said. I wouldn't be who I am without you and this book would be very different.

My cousin Steven died in summer 2022 - "OVER CORRECT" is dedicated to him.

My grandma Jo died in late 2022 - "ALL ANGELS" is dedicated to her. And the rest of the book (not the sexy parts).

Thank you for reading.